52
Simply Powerful
Prayers
for
Christianpreneurs

Tasha "TC" Cooper

UpwardAction® Media
Washington, DC

12/16

Mr. Felix—

Blessings as you
continue to Pray. Act. Trust.
May 2017 be your best
year yet.

TC

DEDICATION

This book is dedicated to ~

Christianpreneurs throughout the world who are putting
in the late nights and early mornings necessary to build
Bible-principled businesses.

.

Table of Contents

ACKNOWLEDGMENTS

I'd like to say thank you to:

My Lord and Savior Jesus Christ. Thank you for showing me again and again and again that I am loved, and all of my experiences are preparing me for today, tomorrow and the days to come.

My parents. Thank you for inspiring me to do the Work I have been called to do.

My sister-friend Marenda. Thank you for blessing me with your positive energy, words of encouragement when I am tired, and sisterhood of more than 20 years.

My family of ACTIONeers from Periscope. Thank you for honoring me with the opportunity to mentor and guide you, as we collectively do Work that is transforming the world.

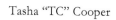
Tasha "TC" Cooper

MY STORY

This is my life work: helping people understand and respond to this Message. It came as a sheer gift to me, a real surprise, God handling all the details.

When it came to presenting the Message to people who had no background in God's way, I was the least qualified of any of the available Christians.

God saw to it that I was equipped, but you can be sure that it had nothing to do with my natural ability.

Ephesians 3:7-8
MSG

Tasha "TC" Cooper

Welcome to 52 Simply Powerful Prayers for Christianpreneurs

Everything you hope to achieve in business and dream of accomplishing in your life is not only available to you, it is waiting for you to arrive. Prayer is the tool God gives each of us to bridge the gap between our dreams and our reality.

This book you are holding in your hands *(or reading on your electronic device)* right now contains bible verses and prayers inspired by God.

These prayers were revealed to me during the course of a long weekend with instructions to share them with YOU, so you might realize the purpose for which God has called you and your business to serve in the world. As in my first bible-based book, 52 Lessons for Christianpreneurs *(available at www.FaithFocusFlow.com)*, I capitalize the word "Work" throughout this book. I do this to symbolize the importance of actions that are inspired by God.

It is my prayer this little book of simply powerful bible-based prayers becomes one of your favorite tools for unlocking God's promises. I hope you'll read these prayers over and over again, memorize them and modify the words to make them your own.

Blessings to you in using prayer + your action to build a business that serves people and honors God. I am praying and cheering for you!

With Love ~ TC

Tasha "TC" Cooper

Instructions for Using this Prayer Book:

This interactive prayer book is designed to ACTIVATE your prayer life. It contains 52 passages of scripture and 52 prayers. There are two different types of prayers in this book.

The first type of prayer is inspired by passages of scripture found on the page right before each prayer *(this is the left side of the printed book)*. These prayers capture the spirit of the passages of scripture without actually quoting the bible.

The second type of prayer contains direct quotes from the scriptures immediately before each prayer. These prayers provide a model for how to strengthen your prayer life by literally praying the words in scripture passages.

I hope you will study these styles of prayer and use them to write your own bible-based prayers that bring the Word of God alive in your life.

Inside of this book, you will also find space to sign your name and write down the date you make each prayer your own by praying it to God. You can sign and date each prayer as many times as you would like in the days, weeks, months and years to come.

Questions?
Email us at Prayers@UpwardAction.com or tweet us at www.Twitter.com/FaithFocusFlow

Oh teach us to count our days
so our minds may learn wisdom.

Psalm 90:12
OEB

A prayer for becoming more intentional.

Dear Lord,

Thank you for this day and for the opportunity to come to you in prayer. I also thank you for _____ _____ _____.

I ask that you help me become more intentional about how I invest every day of my life, for I know my days here on earth are numbered, and my opportunities to share the wisdom I have gained from my business experiences are few.

I make this request in Jesus' name.

Amen.

My Name: _____   Date: _____

David continued to address Solomon:

"Take charge! Take heart!

Don't be anxious or get discouraged.
GOD, my God, is with you in this; he won't walk off
and leave you in the lurch.

He's at your side until every last detail is completed for
conducting the worship of God.

You have all the priests and Levites standing ready to
pitch in, and skillful craftsmen and artisans of every
king ready to go to work.

Both leaders and people are ready.

Just say the word."

1 Chronicles 28:20-21
MSG

A prayer for courage to do what is necessary.

Dear Lord,

Thank you for this day and for the opportunity to come to you in prayer. I also thank you for _____

_____

_____.

I ask that you grant me the courage and heart I need to consistently perform the tasks necessary to create sustainable success in my business, without anxiety or fear that my work will be in vain.

Your Word promises that you are with me, and when I'm doing the Work you have assigned to me, you will not leave me in a lurch.

Thank you for your promises and for your Word.

Amen.

My Name: _____   Date: _____

Do not let your hearts be troubled.

Believe in God; believe also in Me.

John 14:1-2
OEB

A prayer for the ability to defeat fear.

Dear Lord,

Thank you for this day and for the opportunity to come to you in prayer. I also thank you for _____

_____

_____.

I ask that you help me recognize the seeds of fear when they form in my life, and quickly replace all traces of fear with PRAYER and FAITH that my prayers will be answered.

I make this request in Jesus' name.

Amen.

_____   _____

My Name: Date:

Do not be anxious about anything, but in every situation, by prayer and petition, with thanksgiving, present your requests to God.

And the peace of God, which transcends all understanding, will guard your hearts and your minds in Christ Jesus.

Philippians 4:6-7
NIV

A prayer for relief from anxiety.

Dear Lord,

Thank you for this day and for the opportunity to come to you in prayer. I also thank you for _____

_____

_____.

I ask that you remove all anxiety about my company from my consciousness and strengthen my FAITH in your perfect Will.

Help me replace the void created by the removal of all anxiety with consistent <u>imperfect action</u>, for I know that Faith without Works is dead.

I make this request in Jesus' name.

Amen.

My Name: _____   Date: _____

But first seek his kingdom and the righteousness that he requires, and then all these things will be added for you.

Matthew 6:33-34
OEB

A prayer for managing success.

Dear Lord,

Thank you for this day and for the opportunity to come to you in prayer. I also thank you for _____ _____ _____.

In the midst of the success and good fortune I am blessed to enjoy, I ask that you help me remain humble and focused on your Word, for I know all things come from your Grace and Mercy.

I make this request in Jesus' name.

Amen.

My Name: _____   Date: _____

"No weapon forged against you will prevail,
and you will refute every tongue that accuses you.

This is the heritage of the servants of the LORD,
and this is their vindication from me,"
declares the LORD.

Isaiah 54:17
NIV

A prayer for protection in the midst of storms.

Dear Lord,

Thank you for this day and for the opportunity to come to you in prayer. I also thank you for _____
_____
_____.

I ask that you protect me and grant me peace in the midst of the seen and unseen storms raging around me. I know you control the clouds, winds, and rain.

I trust in your promise that no weapon formed against me will prosper.

Thank you for your Word.

Amen.

_____   _____

My Name: Date:

Post this at all the intersections, dear friends:

Lead with your ears, follow up with your tongue, and
let anger straggle along in the rear.

God's righteousness doesn't grow from human anger.

James 1:19-20
MSG

A prayer for a temperament that honors God.

Dear Lord,

Thank you for this day and for the opportunity to come to you in prayer. I also thank you for _____
_____
_____.

I ask that you help me become more quick to hear, slow to speak and slow to anger, for I know my anger does not accomplish your righteousness.

I make this request in Jesus' name.

Amen.

My Name: _____   Date: _____

Put that message into practice,
and do not merely listen to it – deceiving yourself.

James 1:22-23
OEB

A prayer for help in being a Doer.

Dear Lord,

Thank you for this day and for the opportunity to come to you in prayer. I also thank you for _____

_____

_____.

I ask that you help me become not only a hearer of your Word but a DOER of your Word, for I know my business transforms the world when it is <u>doing</u> the Work that you have assigned.

I make this request in Jesus' name.

Amen.

_____   _____

My Name: Date:

God is our refuge and strength,
a very present help in trouble.

So we have no fear, though earth should change,
and hills totter into the heart of the ocean.

Let its waters roar and foam,
let the mountains shake with the swelling thereof.

On our side is the Lord of hosts,
our sure deference is the God of Jacob.
Selah.

Psalm 46:1-3
OEB

A prayer for strength in times of trouble.

Dear Lord,

Thank you for this day and for the opportunity to come to you in prayer. I also thank you for _____

_____

_____.

I ask that you help me find strength in knowing you are my help in times of trouble and my rock in times of success.

Help me stand fearless as I use my influence in business to do the Work that you have called me to do.

I make this request in Jesus' name.

Amen.

_____   _____

My Name: Date:

Actually, I don't have a sense of needing anything personally. I've learned by now to be quite content whatever my circumstances.

I'm just as happy with little as with much, with much as with little. I've found the recipe for being happy whether full or hungry, hands full or hands empty.

Whatever I have, wherever I am, I can make it through anything in the One who makes me who I am.

Philippians 4:11-14
MSG

A prayer for contentment in being of service.

Dear Lord,

Thank you for this day and for the opportunity to come to you in prayer. I also thank you for _____

_____

_____.

I ask that you help me build a business that offers programs, products and services that are a true benefit to our clients and customers. Help us to operate from a place of service, not need.

I trust YOU, Lord, to supply all of our needs.

I make this request in Jesus' name.

Amen.

_____   _____

My Name: Date:

So roll up your sleeves, put your mind in gear,
be totally ready to receive the gift that's coming when
Jesus arrives.

Don't lazily slip back into those old grooves of evil,
doing just what you feel like doing.

You didn't know any better then; you do now.

As obedient children, let yourselves be pulled into a
way of life shaped by God's life, a life energetic and
blazing with holiness.

God said, "I am holy; you be holy."

1 Peter 1:13-16
MSG

A prayer for self-discipline.

Dear Lord,

Thank you for this day and for the opportunity to come to you in prayer. I also thank you for _____ _____ _____.

I ask that you help me prepare my mind for success, become more self-disciplined in my daily actions and keep my hope completely grounded in your Grace.

I make this request in Jesus' name.

Amen.

My Name: _____   Date: _____

So don't lose a minute in building on what you've been given, complementing your basic faith with good character, spiritual understanding, alert discipline, passionate patience, reverent wonder, warm friendliness, and generous love, each dimension fitting into and developing the others.

With these qualities active and growing in your lives, no grass will grow under your feet, no day will pass without its reward as you mature in your experience of our Master Jesus.

Without these qualities you can't see what's right before you, oblivious that your old sinful life has been wiped off the books.

2 Peter 1:5-9
MSG

A prayer for endurance in my pursuit of Godliness.

Dear Lord,

Thank you for this day and for the opportunity to come to you in prayer. I also thank you for _____
_____
_____.

I ask that you help supplement my Faith with goodness, my Goodness with knowledge, my Knowledge with self-control, my Self-control with endurance, and my Endurance with Godliness so your Will can be done through my business endeavors.

I make this request in Jesus' name.

Amen.

My Name: _____   Date: _____

All joy be yours at all times in your union with the Lord.

Again I repeat – All joy be yours.

Philippians 4:4-5
OEB

A prayer for joy through ups and downs in business.

Dear Lord,

Thank you for this day and for the opportunity to come to you in prayer. I also thank you for _____

_____

_____.

I ask that you grant me the presence of mind to rejoice in the goodness of your Grace and Mercy through my every SUCCESS and also what appears to be failure or set-back.

Help me remember that you have commanded all joy be mine. Please also help me become more confident that ALL things are working for my good.

I make this request in Jesus' name.

Amen.

My Name: _____   Date: _____

Whatever you do, do it with all your heart, as if working for the Master and not for people, since you know that it is from the Master that you will receive the inheritance which will be your reward.

You are serving Christ, the Master.

Those who do wrong will reap the wrong they have done.

Colossians 3:23-25
OEB

A prayer for enthusiasm when I am weary.

Dear Lord,

Thank you for this day and for the opportunity to come to you in prayer. I also thank you for _____
_____
_____.

I ask that you renew my passion for the Vision you have placed in my heart and mind. Help me take <u>honorable</u> actions to increase my company's profitability so enthusiastically my positive outlook becomes contagious. Help my spirit and demeanor make it evident to all who encounter me that I am working for your approval.

I make this request in Jesus' name.

Amen.

_____   _____
My Name: Date:

Teach believers with your life:
by word, by demeanor, by love, by faith, by integrity.

Stay at your post reading scripture,
giving counsel, teaching.

1 Timothy 4:12
MSG

A prayer for a demeanor that honors God.

Dear Lord,

Thank you for this day and for the opportunity to come to you in prayer. I also thank you for _____

_____

_____.

Let my words, conduct, love, spirit and faith in serving you through my business endeavors be an example of your faithfulness to both (i) those who believe in you and (ii) those who do not yet believe.

Let everyone who encounters me see your love for humanity through me.

I make this request in Jesus' name.

Amen.

_____   _____

My Name: Date:

Isaac planted crops in that land
and the same year reaped a hundredfold,
because the LORD blessed him.

Genesis 26:12
NIV

A prayer for consistency in taking the right actions.

Dear Lord,

Thank you for this day and for the opportunity to come to you in prayer. I also thank you for _____
_____
_____.

I ask that you help me bountifully sow into people and opportunities that will take me to new levels of success.

Help me consistently ACT upon my knowledge that an essential part of sowing bountifully is giving a portion of what I have earned back to you *(through the Church)*.

I trust that what I sow bountifully, I will reap generously at your *(not my)* designated time. *Although …* *I pray your time will be expeditious.* ☺

Amen.

_____   _____
My Name: Date:

So let's do it – full of belief,
confident that we're presentable inside and out.

Let's keep a firm grip
on the promises that keep us going.
He always keeps his word.

Hebrews 10:22-23
MSG

A prayer for confidence in God's promises.

Dear Lord,

Thank you for this day and for the opportunity to come to you in prayer. I also thank you for _____

_____

_____.

I ask that you help me move forward in the direction of the Vision you have given me, full of belief and confidence that your promises to me will be fulfilled.

Amen.

_____   _____
My Name: Date:

Do you want to stand out?
Then step down.
Be a servant.

If you puff yourself up,
you'll get the wind knocked out of you.

But if you're content to simply be yourself,
your life will count for plenty.

Matthew 23:11-12
MSG

A prayer for humbleness in seasons of abundance.

Dear Lord,

Thank you for this day and for the opportunity to come to you in prayer. I also thank you for _____

_____

_____.

As I celebrate the abundance you have bestowed upon me, please help me maintain a servant's heart so I remain blessed, highly favored and your beacon of light for those in darkness.

Please help me always remember that "those who exalt themselves will be humbled, and those who humble themselves will be exalted." *Matthew 23:12*

I make this request in Jesus' name.

Amen.

_____   _____

My Name: Date:

Do not judge and you will not be judged.

* * * * *

A good measure, pressed down, shaken together and running over, will be poured into your lap.

For with the measure you use,
it will be measured to you.

Excerpts from Luke 6:37-38
NIV

A prayer for release from judgment.

Dear Lord,

Thank you for this day and for the opportunity to come to you in prayer. I also thank you for _____

_____

_____.

As I move about my day, please help me become intentional about not judging others, so you will not judge me.

I make this request in Jesus' name.

Amen.

My Name: _____   Date: _____

Do not condemn and you will not be condemned.

* * * * *

A good measure, pressed down, shaken together and running over, will be poured into your lap.

For with the measure you use,
it will be measured to you.

Excerpts from Luke 6:37-38
NIV

A prayer for release from condemnation.

Dear Lord,

Thank you for this day and for the opportunity to come to you in prayer. I also thank you for _____

_____

_____.

As I move about my day, please help me resist any and all temptation to condemn anyone, so you will not condemn me.

I make this request in Jesus' name.

Amen.

My Name: _____

Date: _____

Forgive and you will be forgiven.

Give, and it will be given unto you.

* * * * *

A good measure, pressed down, shaken together and running over, will be poured into your lap.

For with the measure you use,
it will be measured to you.

Excerpts from Luke 6:37-38
NIV

A prayer for the ability to forgive.

Dear Lord,

Thank you for this day and for the opportunity to come to you in prayer. I also thank you for _____

_____

_____.

As I move about my day, please help me forgive everyone whom I feel has wronged me in business and life, for I want you to forgive me of all my sins.

I make this request in Jesus' name.

Amen.

_____   _____

My Name: Date:

Pay close attention friend,
to what your father tells you;
Never forget what you learned
at your mother's knee.

Wear their counsel like flowers in your hair,
Like rings on your fingers.

Proverbs 1:8-9
MSG

A prayer for help being a better listener.

Dear Lord,

Thank you for this day and for the opportunity to come to you in prayer. I also thank you for _____ _____ _____.

I ask that you help me hear your instructions clearly and adhere to your teachings for how to run my business.

Help me better listen and follow the wisdom shared with me by experienced business owners and help me block out all chatter from others.

I make this request in Jesus' name.

Amen.

My Name: _____

Date: _____

When we trust in him,
We're free to say whatever needs to be said,
Bold to go wherever we need to go.

Ephesians 3:12
MSG

A prayer for more confidence and boldness.

Dear Lord,

Thank you for this day and for the opportunity to come to you in prayer. I also thank you for _____ _____ _____.

I ask that you help me become more confident and bold in saying whatever needs to be said, and doing whatever needs to be done to build a business that supports clients, customers and staff in a way that reflects your grace and mercy.

I make this request in Jesus' name.

Amen.

My Name: _____   Date: _____

Anyone on God's side listens to God's words.

This is why you're not listening –
because you're not on God's side.

John 8:47
MSG

A prayer for a clear mind and heart.

Dear Lord,

Thank you for this day and for the opportunity to come to you in prayer. I also thank you for _____
_____
_____.

I ask that you open my ears and clear my mind, so I can listen carefully and hear your voice.

Then, please give me the discipline and stamina I need to take the actions you have commanded.

I make this request in Jesus' name.

Amen.

_____   _____

My Name: Date:

Now that you have done with all malice,
all deceitfulness, insincerity, jealous feelings,
and all backbiting,
like newly born infants, **crave pure spiritual milk,**
so that you may be enabled by it to grow until you
attain salvation – since "you have found by experience
that the Lord is kind."

1 Peter 2:1-4
OEB

A prayer for release from negative thoughts.

Dear Lord,

Thank you for this day and for the opportunity to come to you in prayer. I also thank you for _____

_____

_____.

Please rid my heart, mind and tongue of all malice, deceitfulness, insincerity and jealous feelings in business dealings.

Help me build my company on Godly principles, and let my words and actions inspire others to do the same.

I make this request in Jesus' name.

Amen.

My Name: _____   Date: _____

In all your ways submit to him,
and he will make your paths straight.

Proverbs 3:6
NIV

A prayer for help using my business to acknowledge God.

Dear Lord,

Thank you for this day and for the opportunity to come to you in prayer. I also thank you for _____

_____

_____.

I ask that you direct my actions so in all of my business practices I am acknowledging you, for I know when I do this, you will make my path straight.

I make this request in Jesus' name.

Amen.

_____   _____

My Name: Date:

If GOD doesn't build the house,
The builders only build shacks.

If GOD doesn't guard the city,
the night watchman might as well nap.

It's useless to rise early and go to bed late,
and work your worried fingers to the bone.

Don't you know he enjoys
giving rest to those he loves?

Psalm 127:1
MSG

A prayer for God's presence.

Dear Lord,

Thank you for this day and for the opportunity to come to you in prayer. I also thank you for _____

_____

_____.

I ask that you be present in my every decision and action, for I know unless you are active in the building of my business, the effort it takes to build it is in vain.

And, unless you watch over the delivery of our programs, products and services, my company's work is in vain.

I know you love me, and so I make this request in Jesus' name.

Amen.

My Name: _____   Date: _____

The LORD is my shepherd, I lack nothing.

He makes me lie down in green pastures,
he leads me beside quiet waters,
he refreshes my soul.

He guides me along the right paths
for his name's sake.

Psalm 23:1-3
NIV

A prayer for increased awareness of my assets.

Dear Lord,

Thank you for this day and for the opportunity to come to you in prayer. I also thank you for _____ _____ _____.

As I move throughout the day, please help me be fully aware that I have everything needed to manage and grow a profitable business that honors you.

Let me never forget you are my shepherd, you make me to lie down in green pastures, you lead me beside the still waters and you restore my soul.

Thank you, Lord, for guiding me along the right paths of building a Christ-centered business.

Amen.

_____   _____
My Name: Date:

He said to them:

"It is not for you to know the times or dates the Father has set by his own authority. But you will receive power when the Holy Spirit comes on you; and you will be my witnesses in Jerusalem, and in all Judea and Samaria, and to the end of the earth."

Acts 1: 7-8
NIV

A prayer for trust in God's timing.

Dear Lord,

Thank you for this day and for the opportunity to come to you in prayer. I also thank you for _____
_____
_____.

As I move throughout my day, help me feel peace in knowing regardless of what is happening around me, the success I desire will happen at your appointed time.

I rejoice in knowing my success in business will be a shining example that through the power of the Holy Spirit, all things are possible.

I make this request in Jesus' name.

Amen.

My Name: _____   Date: _____

Do to others whatever you would wish them to do to you; for that is the teaching of both the Law and the prophets.

Matthew 7:12-13
OEB

A prayer for increased ability to give.

Dear Lord,

Thank you for this day and for the opportunity to come to you in prayer. I also thank you for _____

_____

_____.

I ask that you help me become intentional about doing for my clients, customers, vendors, colleagues and even my competitors what I want others to do for me, not because I expect anything in return, but because this is what you have commanded me to do.

I make this request in Jesus' name.

Amen.

My Name: _____   Date: _____

So let us exult in our hope
of attaining God's glorious ideal.

And not only that, but let us also exult in our troubles;
for we know that trouble develops endurance,
and endurance strength of character,
and strength of character hope,
and that 'Hope never disappoints.'

Romans 5:2-5
OEB

A prayer for perseverance.

Dear Lord,

Thank you for this day and for the opportunity to come to you in prayer. I also thank you for _____

_____

_____.

I ask for the presence of mind to always seek and find your glory in my business experiences. I reaffirm my trust that whatever comes my way has been allowed by you to increase my ability to persevere, strengthen my character, and give me hope - for these things are essential for business builders like me.

I make this request in Jesus' name.

Amen.

_____   _____

My Name: Date:

When I was a child,
I talked like a child,
I thought like a child,
I reasoned like a child.
When I became a [wo]man,
I put the ways of childhood behind me

1 Corinthians 13:11
NIV

A prayer for wisdom.

Dear Lord,

Thank you for this day and for the opportunity to come
to you in prayer. I also thank you for _____
_____
_____.

I ask that you grant me wisdom to make thoughtful
business decisions as a seasoned expert *(and help me seek
wise counsel when necessary)* instead of chasing "the latest
and greatest" thing in the marketplace like a child.

I make this request in Jesus' name.

Amen.

My Name: _____   Date: _____

Good leaders cultivate honest speech;
They love advisors who tell them the truth.

Proverbs 16:13
MSG

A prayer for the ability to speak wise words.

Dear Lord,

Thank you for this day and for the opportunity to come to you in prayer. I also thank you for _____

_____

_____.

I ask that you cultivate my speech so I become a better leader for my clients, customers, vendors and staff.

I make this request in Jesus' name.

Amen.

_____   _____

My Name: Date:

We must do the works of him who sent me, while it is day; night is coming, when no one can work.

As long as I am in the world, I am the light of the world.

John 9:4-6
OEB

A prayer for proper action in the right season.

Dear Lord,

Thank you for this day and for the opportunity to come to you in prayer. I also thank you for _____
_____
_____.

Please direct my path so I am a light in the world – actively using my skills, talents and gifts to do the Work you have called me to do, for I know my ability to work will not last forever.

I make this request in Jesus' name.

Amen.

_____   _____

My Name: Date:

Rather encourage one another daily – while there is a 'Today' – to prevent anyone among you from being hardened by the deceitfulness of sin.

For we now all share in the Christ, if indeed we retain, unshaken to the end, the confidence that we had at the first.

Hebrews 3:13-15
OEB

A prayer for my staff.

Dear Lord,

Thank you for this day and for the opportunity to come to you in prayer. I also thank you for _____

_____

_____.

I ask that you direct me to the members of my team whom you want me to encourage this week. Let my actions show my business practices are guided by you.

Please also let my words be encouraging and empowering so my team is inspired to be their best.

I make this request in Jesus' name.

Amen.

_____   _____
My Name: Date:

Let us vie with one another in a rivalry of love and
noble actions.

And let us not, as some do, cease to meet together;
but, on the contrary, let us encourage one another,
and all the more, now that you see the day is drawing
near.

Hebrews 10:24-16
OEB

A prayer for my vendors.

Dear Lord,

Thank you for this day and for the opportunity to come to you in prayer. I also thank you for _____

_____

_____.

I ask that you direct me to the vendors you want me to encourage this week. Let my actions show that my company is led by you.

Let my words be encouraging and empowering so the vendors who support us are inspired to implement business practices that reflect your Grace and Mercy.

I make this request in Jesus' name.

Amen.

_____   _____
My Name: Date:

But if serving the LORD seems undesirable to you,
then choose for yourselves this day
whom you will serve ...

But as for me and my household,
we will serve the Lord.

Joshua 24:15
NIV

A prayer for direction.

Dear Lord,

Thank you for this day and for the opportunity to come to you in prayer. I also thank you for _____

_____

_____.

I ask that you guide my actions so it is clear that as for my business and me, we adhere to standards that honor and serve you.

I make this request in Jesus' name.

Amen.

_____   _____

My Name: Date:

Above all else, guard your heart,
for everything you do flows from it.

Proverbs 4:23
NIV

A prayer for God to protect my heart.

Dear Lord,

Thank you for this day and for the opportunity to come to you in prayer. I also thank you for _____ _____ _____.

I ask that you guard my heart as I continue to pursue the vision for my business you have given me.

Help me remain encouraged and inspired, knowing you are leading the way to increased profitability and sustainable success.

I make this request in Jesus' name.

Amen.

My Name: _____   Date: _____

Do not let us grow vain,
and provoke or envy one another.

My friends, even if someone should be caught
committing a sin, you who are spiritually minded
should, in a gentle spirit, help them to recover
themselves, taking care that you yourselves are not
tempted.

Bear one another's burdens, and so carry out the Law
of the Christ.

If a person imagines themselves to be somebody, when
they are really nobody, they deceive themselves.

Let everyone test their own work, and then their cause
for satisfaction will be in themselves and not in a
comparison with their neighbor; for everyone must
carry their own load.

The person, however, who is being instructed in the
message ought always to share their blessings with their
teacher.

Galatians 6:1-6
OEB

A prayer for discipline in my actions.

Dear Lord,

Thank you for this day and for the opportunity to come to you in prayer. I also thank you for _____

_____

_____.

I ask that you help me take the right actions to develop programs, products, and services that serve our clients and customers by eliminating all burdens and problems that my company can resolve.

Please let my company's Work be a blessing to those we serve, as well as those who are served by the people we serve.

I make this request in Jesus' name.

Amen.

_____   _____

My Name: Date:

This day is the Lord's own creation:
in it let us joy and be glad.

Psalm 118:24
OEB

A prayer for a spirit of thanksgiving.

Dear Lord,

Thank you for this day and for the opportunity to come to you in prayer. I also thank you for _____

_____

_____.

I ask that you help me appreciate and rejoice in every day, for every day is a day you have made, and every moment presents an opportunity to be better than I was the moment before.

I make this request in Jesus' name.

Amen.

_____   _____

My Name: Date:

Summing it all up, friends,
I'd say you'll do best by filling your minds
and meditating on things true, noble, reputable,
authentic, compelling, gracious –
the best, not the worst;
the beautiful, not the ugly;
things to praise, not things to curse.

Philippians 4:8
MSG

A prayer for guidance as I meditate on God's Word.

Dear Lord,

Thank you for this day and for the opportunity to come to you in prayer. I also thank you for _____

_____

_____.

I ask that you guide me in meditating only on those things that are true, noble, just, pure, lovely, of good report, virtuous and praiseworthy in my business.

Help me eject all other thoughts from my mind.

I make this request in Jesus' name.

Amen.

_____   _____

My Name: Date:

But those who hope in the LORD
will renew their strength.

They will soar on wings like eagles;
They will run and not grow weary,
They will walk and not be faint.

Isaiah 40:31
NIV

A prayer for patience.

Dear Lord,

Thank you for this day and for the opportunity to come to you in prayer. I also thank you for _____
_____
_____.

I ask that you help me WAIT on you for I know you shall renew my strength.

I believe and trust you will send the Holy Spirit to fuel my spirit at the right time, so I can run and not be weary.

I pray that as I pursue my business endeavors, you will grant me endurance so I do not faint.

I make this request in Jesus' name.

Amen.

_____   _____

My Name: Date:

But thanks be to God, who gives us the victory,
through Jesus Christ, our Lord.

Therefore, my dear friends, stand firm, unshaken,
always diligent in the Lord's work, for you know that,
in union with him, your toil is not in vain.

1 Corinthians 15:57-58
OEB

A prayer for strength and courage.

Dear Lord,

Thank you for this day and for the opportunity to come to you in prayer. I also thank you for _____

_____

_____.

I ask that you help me become strong, wise and courageous enough to make the right decisions for growing my company using ethical principles.

Release me from all fear and increase my trust in you.

Help me remember that You, my God, are with me, and my Work to build a Christ-centered business is not in vain.

I make this request in Jesus' name.

Amen.

_____   _____

My Name: Date:

For I know the plans I have for you,
declares the LORD,
plans to prosper you and not to harm you,
plans to give you hope and a future.

Jeremiah 29:11
NIV

A prayer for faith in my future.

Dear Lord,

Thank you for this day and for the opportunity to come to you in prayer. I also thank you for _____
_____
_____.

I ask that you help me always remember that regardless of what is happening in my life and business right now, you have plans to prosper me and not harm me.

Please help me take smart actions that move me towards the hope and future you have for not only me and my company today, but also my future generations to come.

I make this request in Jesus' name.

Amen.

_____   _____

My Name: Date:

"Then you will call on me and come and pray to me,
and I will listen to you. You will seek me and find me
when you seek me with all your heart.

I will be found by you," declares the LORD,
"and will bring you back from captivity.

I will gather you from all the nations and places where I
have banished you," declares the LORD,
"and will bring you back to the place from which I
carried you into exile."

Jeremiah 29:12-14
NIV

A prayer for increased discipline.

Dear Lord,

Thank you for this day and for the opportunity to come to you in prayer. I also thank you for _____
_____
_____.

I ask that you help me become more disciplined in coming to you in daily prayer.

I pray that you hear my prayers and, so long as I do my part, you will bring my business ventures into a long season of sustainable growth.

I make this request in Jesus' name.

Amen.

_____   _____
My Name: Date:

Jesus looked at them and said,
"With people this is impossible,
but with God everything is possible."

Matthew 19:26-27
OEB

A prayer for increased focus.

Dear Lord,

Thank you for this day and for the opportunity to come to you in prayer. I also thank you for _____
_____
_____.

I ask that you grant me the wisdom necessary to transform the Vision you have placed in my heart into my reality.

Help me fully trust and believe that through YOU all things are possible.

I make this request in Jesus' name.

Amen.

_____   _____
My Name: Date:

How much better to get wisdom than gold,
To get insight rather than silver.

Proverbs 16:16
NIV

A prayer for wisdom and understanding.

Dear Lord,

Thank you for this day and for the opportunity to come
to you in prayer. I also thank you for _____
_____
_____.

I ask that you help me approach every situation I
encounter in a way that gives me the insight necessary
to increase my company's revenue, using strategies and
tactics that honor you.

I make this request in Jesus' name.

Amen.

_____   _____

My Name: Date:

We have different gifts,
according to the grace given to each of us.

If your gift is prophesying,
then prophesy in accordance with your faith;
if it is serving, then serve;
if it is teaching, then teach;
if it is to encourage, then give encouragement;
if it is giving, then give generously;
if it is to lead, do it diligently;
if it is to show mercy, do it cheerfully.

Romans 12:6-8
NIV

A prayer for revelation in God's Word.

Dear Lord,

Thank you for this day and for the opportunity to come to you in prayer. I also thank you for _____

_____

_____.

I ask that you help me use my gifts to take my business to new levels of success in a way that honors you and magnifies your name.

I make this request in Jesus' name.

Amen.

My Name: _____ Date: _____

Commit to the LORD whatever you do,
and he will establish your plans.

Proverbs 16:3
NIV

A prayer for help in establishing Godly plans.

Dear Lord,

Thank you for this day and for the opportunity to come to you in prayer. I also thank you for _____

_____

_____.

Lord, I commit the hopes and dreams I have for my company to you, asking you to establish my plans.

I trust and believe that whatever plans are established in your name will be accomplished.

I make this request in Jesus' name.

Amen.

_____   _____

My Name: Date:

Remember the wonders he did, his portents,
the judgments he uttered.

Psalm 105:5
OEB

A prayer for wonders and miracles.

Dear Lord,

Thank you for this day and for the opportunity to come to you in prayer. I also thank you for _____

_____

_____.

I ask that you unleash your wonders, miracles and blessings upon my business endeavors.

I make this request in Jesus' name.

Amen.

_____   _____

My Name: Date:

So Jesus went on to say to those who had believed him:

"If you remain constant to my message,
you are truly my disciples;
and you find out the truth,
and the truth will set you free."

John 8:31-32
OEB

A prayer for increased business acumen.

Dear Lord,

Thank you for this day and for the opportunity to come to you in prayer. I also thank you for _____

_____

_____.

I ask that you help me fully see the truth in my business operations and practices - so I am equipped to do what is necessary to reduce expenses and increase profits.

I make this request in Jesus' name.

Amen.

_____

My Name: Date:

Trust in the LORD with all your heart
and lean not on your own understanding.

Proverbs 3:6
NIV

A prayer for consistency.

Dear Lord,

Thank you for this day and for the opportunity to come to you in prayer. I also thank you for _____
_____
_____.

I ask that you help me consistently implement strategies and tactics necessary to achieve sustainable success.

Please bless the Work of my business beyond my *understanding* of what is possible, and even beyond my wildest dreams.

I make this request in Jesus' name.

Amen.

_____   _____

My Name: Date:

APPENDIX

1. Psalm 90:12 (OEB)
2. 1 Chronicles 28:20-21 (MSG)
3. John 14:1-2 (OEB)
4. Philippians 4:6-7 (NIV)
5. Matthew 6:33-34 (OEB)
6. Isaiah 54:17 (NIV)
7. James 1:19-20 (MSG)
8. James 1:22-23 (OEB)
9. Psalm 46:1-3 (OEB)
10. Philippians 4:11-14 (MSG)
11. 1 Peter 1:13-16 (MSG)
12. 2 Peter 1:5-9 (MSG)
13. Philippians 4:4-5 (OEB)
14. Colossians 3:23-25 (OEB)
15. 1 Timothy 4:12 (MSG)
16. Genesis 26:12 (NIV)
17. Hebrews 10:22-23 (MSG)
18. Matthew 23:11-12 (MSG)
19. Luke 6:37-38 (NIV)
20. Luke 6:37-38 (NIV)
21. Luke 6:37-38 (NIV)
22. Proverbs 1:8-9 (MSG)
23. Ephesians 3:12 (MSG)
24. John 8:47 (MSG)
25. 1 Peter 2:1-4 (OEB)
26. Proverbs 3:6 (NIV)
27. Psalm 127:1 (MSG)
28. Psalm 23:1-3 (NIV)
29. Acts 1:7-8 (NIV)

30. Matthew 7:12-13   (OEB)
31. Romans 5:2-5   (OEB)
32. 1 Corinthians 13:11   (NIV)
33. Proverbs 16:13   (MSG)
34. John 9:4-6   (OEB)
35. Hebrew 3:13-14   (OEB)
36. Hebrews 10:24-26   (OEB)
37. Joshua 24:15   (NIV)
38. Proverbs 4:23   (NIV)
39. Galatians 6:1-6   (OEB)
40. Psalm 118:24   (OEB)
41. Philippians 4:8   (MSG)
42. Isaiah 40:31   (NIV)
43. 1 Corinthians 15:57-58   (OEB)
44. Jeremiah 29:11   (NIV)
45. Jeremiah 29:12-14   (NIV)
46. Matthew 19:26-27   (OEB)
47. Proverbs 16:16   (NIV)
48. Romans 12:6-8   (NIV)
49. Proverbs 16:3   (NIV)
50. Psalm 105:5   (OEB)
51. John 8:31-32   (OEB)
52. Proverbs 3:6   (NIV)

Be sure to add all of these great UpwardAction® Media titles to your business building library.

Increase Your Impact, Influence & Income with Social Marketing

52 Lessons for Chrstianpreneurs

A SMART Goal Daily Planner

All titles by Tasha "TC" Cooper

These and other great professional development resources from UpwardAction®, FaithFocusFlow™ and TC Cooper are available at

www.UpwardActionMedia.com

Join Our Online Community!

When you join our online community, you will get FREE inspirational messages and tools to help you build a business based on biblical principles.

www.FaithFocusFlow.com/Join

Let's Connect!

Facebook
www.Facebook.com/FaithFocusFlow

Twitter
www.Twitter.com/FaithFocusFlow

Instagram
www.Instagram.com/FaithFocusFlow

Book TC Cooper *for* Speaking Engagements

Upward Action LLC
www.UpwardAction.com
WeCare@UpwardAction.com
(800) 753-6576

ABOUT THE AUTHOR

Tasha (TC) Cooper is a Christianpreneur, attorney, best selling author and professional speaker. She serves as president of the award winning social marketing advisory UpwardAction®, and founder of the #CooperZone™ Social Media Training Academies. The #CooperZone™ academies include on-demand video-based training programs that teach professionals *(e.g., lawyers, IT consultants, business coaches and experts)* and their teams how to leverage the power of LinkedIn, Twitter, Facebook, live streaming, digital automation and social marketing to increase impact, expand influence and diversify income.

TC has developed a strong reputation for helping professional service companies and firms use social media and technology to build sustainable business processes that increase profitability.

She is also the author of the Amazon #1 best seller, 52 Lessons for Christianpreneurs. You can learn more about TC, her books, and her Work at **www.TashaCooper.com**.

Made in the USA
San Bernardino, CA
21 December 2016